"Meditation is the key for opening the doors of mysteries."

Abdú'l-Bahá

The Persian Alphabet

We want to simplify your Persian learning journey as it is such a unique & enigmatic language. There are 32 official Persian letters. The letters change form depending on their position in a word or when they appear separate from other letters. For example, the letter ghayn غ has four ways of being written depending on where it appears in any given word:

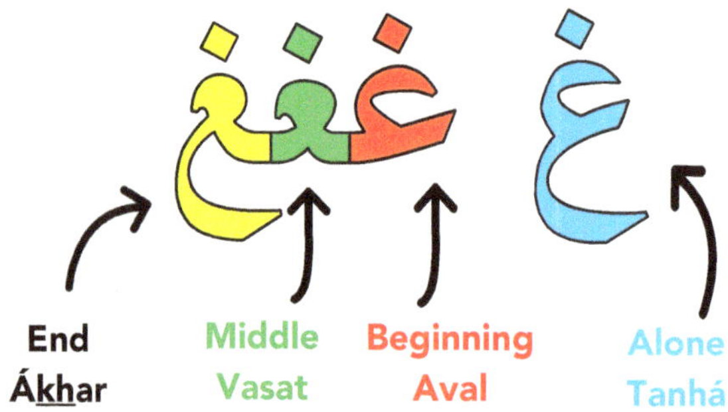

It is important to note that Persian books are read from right to left (←).
There are 7 separate/stand-alone letters that do not connect in the same way to adjacent letters (these will be depicted in blue). They are:

The short vowels a, i & u are usually omitted in literature and are depicted by markings above & below letters (ـــَـــِـــُـ). They are not allocated a letter name, unlike their long vowel counterparts á: alef, í: ye & ú: váv (آ ی و).

Englisi	Farsi
A a	اَ ـَـ ـَـ 'alef
Á á	آ ا ا 'alef
B b	ب ببب Be
D d	د دد dál
F f	ف ففف fe
G g	گ گگگ gáf
H h	ه ههه he
H h	ح ححح he
I i	اِ ـِـ ـِـ
Í í	ی ییی ye
J j	ج ججج jim
K k	ک ککک káf
L l	ل للل lám

Englisi	Farsi
M m	م ممم mím
N n	ن ننن nún
P p	پ پپپ pe
Q q	ق ققق qáf
R r	ر رر re
S s	س سسس sin
S s	ص صصص sád
Th th	ث ثثث se
T t	ت تتت te
T t	ط ططط tá
U u	اُ ـُـ ـُـ
Ú ú	و وو váv
V v	و وو váv

Englisi	Farsi
Y y	ی ییی ye
Dh dh	ذ ذذ zál
D d	ض ضضض zád
Z z	ز زز ze
Z z	ظ ظظظ zá
Ch ch	چ چچچ che
Gh gh	غ غغغ ghayn
Kh kh	خ خخخ khe
Sh sh	ش ششش shín
Zh zh	ژ ژژ zhe
'	ع ععع ayn

Letter Guide©

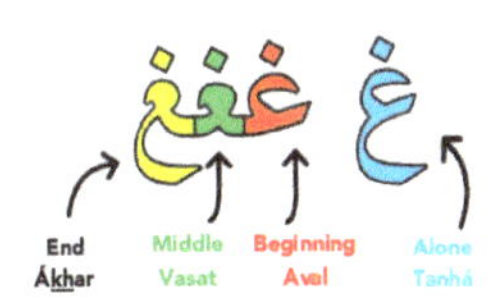

آرى عَليا وَ اَميليا

May you always find comfort & solace in the Divine.

User Guide

Farsi	Englisi	Pronunciation
اَ	a	ant
آ	á	arm
ب	b	bat
د	d	dog
ف	f	fast
گ	g	go
ه	h	hat
ح	h	hat
اِ	i	best
ی	í	meet
ج	j	jet
ک	k	key
ل	l	love
م	m	mint
ن	n	nap
پ	p	pat
ق	q*	merci
ر	r	run
س	s	sand
ص	s	sand
ث	s	sand

Farsi	Englisi	Pronunciation
ت	th	tool
ط	t	tool
اُ	u	short
و	ú	moon
و	v	verb
ی	y	yes
ذ	dh	zero
ض	d	zero
ز	z	zero
ظ	z	zero
چ	ch	chair
غ	gh*	merci
خ	kh*	bach
ش	sh	share
ژ	zh	pleasure
ع	‘	uh-oh†

Vowels

اَ	a	ant
آ	á	arm
اِ	i	best
ی	í	meet
اُ	u	short
و	ú	moon

* guttural sound from back of throat

† Glottal stop, breathing pause

هُوَالله خُدایا

هِدایَت نَما

حِفظ فَرما

سِراجِ روشَن کُن

سِتارهٔ دِرَخشَندهِ نَما

توئی مُقتَدِر

وَ تَوانا.

ع ع

O God,

هُوَالله خُدایا,

Guide me,

هِدايَت نَما

Protect me,

حِفظ فَرما

make of me a shining lamp

سِراجِ روشَن کُن

and a brilliant star.

سِتارهٔ دِرَخشَندِه نَما

Thou art the Mighty

تویُی مُقتَدِر

and the Powerful.

وَ تَوانا. ع ع

***"O God,
guide me,
protect me,
make of me a shining lamp
and a brilliant star.***

***Thou art the Mighty
and the Powerful."***

Abdú'l-Bahá

هُوَ الله خُدایا

هِدایَت نَما

حِفظ فَرما

سِراجِ روشَن کُن

سِتارهٔ دِرَخشَندهِ نَما

توِیی مُقتَدِر

وَ ثَوانا.

٤٤

---

www.ingramcontent.com/pod-product-compliance
Ingram Content Group UK Ltd.
Pitfield, Milton Keynes, MK11 3LW, UK
UKHW060119010826
14089UKWH00005B/55

9 780645 205398